ROGER WILLIAMS UNIVERSITY LIBRARY

CURRICULUM  W9-BLV-564

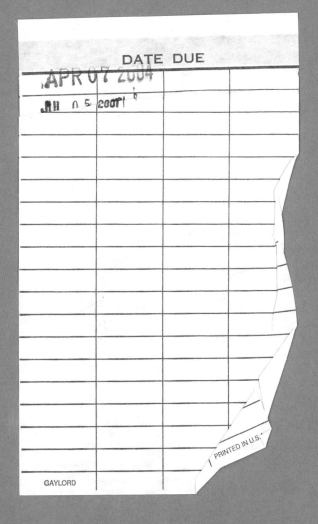

DATE DUE

APR 07 2004			
JUN 0 5 2004			
		PRINTED IN U.S.	
GAYLORD			

ROGER WILLIAMS UNIV. LIBRARY

Sea Critters

by **Sylvia A. Earle**

with photographs by

Wolcott Henry

NATIONAL GEOGRAPHIC SOCIETY
WASHINGTON, D.C.

CMC
QL
122.2
E27
2000

4393663   1/04

CMC QL122.2 .E27 2000
Earle, Sylvia A., 1935-
Sea critters

Published by the National Geographic Society
1145 17th St. N.W.
Washington, D. C. 20036

All rights reserved. Reproduction of the whole or any part of the contents
without written permission from the publisher is prohibited.

Text copyright © 2000 Sylvia A. Earle
Photographs (except as otherwise credited) copyright © 2000 Wolcott Henry

Artwork copyright © 2000 National Geographic Society

Photo on pages 3–4 by Hannah Bernard of the Hawaii Wildlife Fund

Book design by Patrick Collins

To create his artwork, Warren Cutler used watercolor with occasional colored pencil.

The text is set in Palatino with title text in Amigo.

The world's largest nonprofit scientific and educational
organization, the National Geographic Society was founded in 1888
"for the increase and diffusion of geographic knowledge." Since then
it has supported scientific exploration and spread information
to its more than nine million members worldwide. The
National Geographic Society educates and inspires millions
every day through magazines, books, television programs, videos,
maps and atlases, research grants, the National Geographic Bee,
teacher workshops, and innovative classroom materials.

The Society is supported through membership dues and
income from the sale of its educational products.
Call 1-800-NGS-LINE (647-5463) for more information.
Visit our Web site: www.nationalgeographic.com

Library of Congress Catalog Number: 00-026875

ISBN 0-7922-7181-5

Printed in the United States of America

Front cover: A glowing nudibranch, or sea slug, inches across the ocean floor (see pages 12–13).
Title page: A starfish nestles among the coral formations of a reef.

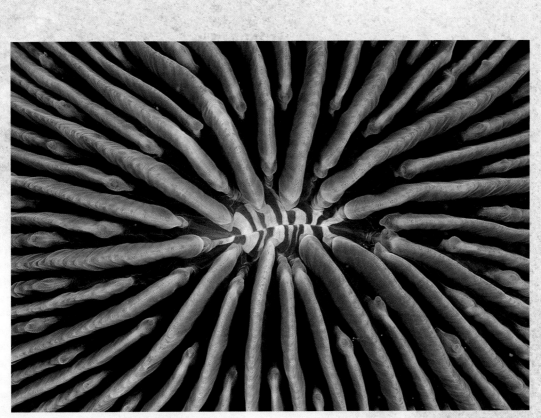

PLATE CORAL

To all who love and care for sea critters, especially Russell,
Kevin, Taylor, and Morgan
—Sylvia A. Earle

To my family and friends with thanks for all your support
—Wolcott Henry

Introduction

Water is magical! All creatures, large and small, must have it, from those living in the deepest seas to those who live in the highest trees. Nearly all of Earth's water—97 percent—is ocean. It's an ocean filled with life! Sea critters abound, making every spoonful a kind of living soup. Of the more than 30 great divisions of animal life, most can be found in the sea. Only about half have homes on land. Some of the largest animals ever—whales, giant squid, huge jellies, big sharks—are in the ocean, but most life in the sea is small, smaller than your thumb! If we could travel back in time to see the world long before there were trees or dinosaurs or frogs or birds or dogs or people—hundreds of millions of years ago—we would find in the ocean sea stars and jellyfish, sponges and crabs, and even some strange-looking fish. They are among Earth's pioneers. Come now and meet some of their descendants: sea critters, some large, some small, but all part of what makes the ocean alive.

HUMPBACK WHALE with CALF

Animals with Holes

Imagine sitting in one place for most of your life with tasty morsels brought to you by the surrounding sea. That's what sponges do. Sponges—the animals with holes—are called PORIFERA. Water flows through hundreds of tiny holes all over the sponge's body, then squirts out through a big hole—or sometimes lots of big holes—at the top. Sponges come in many colors, from red to bright blue to gold to clear like glass. Some are tiny, no bigger than the nail on your littlest finger. Others, such as the barrel sponge in the photograph, can grow large enough for you to sit in with room to spare. Sponges have no brains, but they have lived in the sea for at least 500 million years. They must be doing something right!

BASKET SPONGE

GLASS SPONGE

FINGER SPONGE

◄ BARREL SPONGE

The Stingers

Jellyfish, corals, anemones—the stingers—
are in the group CNIDARIA. All
have a simple plan for living.
Most rely on tiny stinging cells
in their many tentacles to stun
shrimp, little fish, and other
small sea creatures before
gobbling them down.
Jellyfish pulse along with
ocean currents. Their soft

JELLYFISH

bodies feel like gelatin, slick and smooth.
Anemones are like jellies upside down, with
tentacles crowning a muscular
body. Corals, such as the ones
shown here, cluster together.
Some kinds join together by
the hundreds or thousands and

**SEA
ANEMONE**

build a common home—the coral
reef. Coral reefs are like cities,
where millions of creatures live together
among the coral's nooks and crannies.

◀ CUP CORAL

Worms

Many kinds of worms live in the sea: ANNELIDS, NEMATODES, and more. Some are flat, some are round, but most are long and slim. Some have bristly legs; others are sleek and smooth, like earthworms. Many have beautiful, lacy tentacles, such as the Christmas-tree worm. Some kinds of worms, when they get together, look like oodles of noodles! Worms have hearts (sometimes several) and stomachs, and all have muscles. Most worms are very small, but others grow to six feet tall.

PURPLE FLATWORM

GIANT BRISTLE WORM

CHRISTMAS TREE WORMS ▶

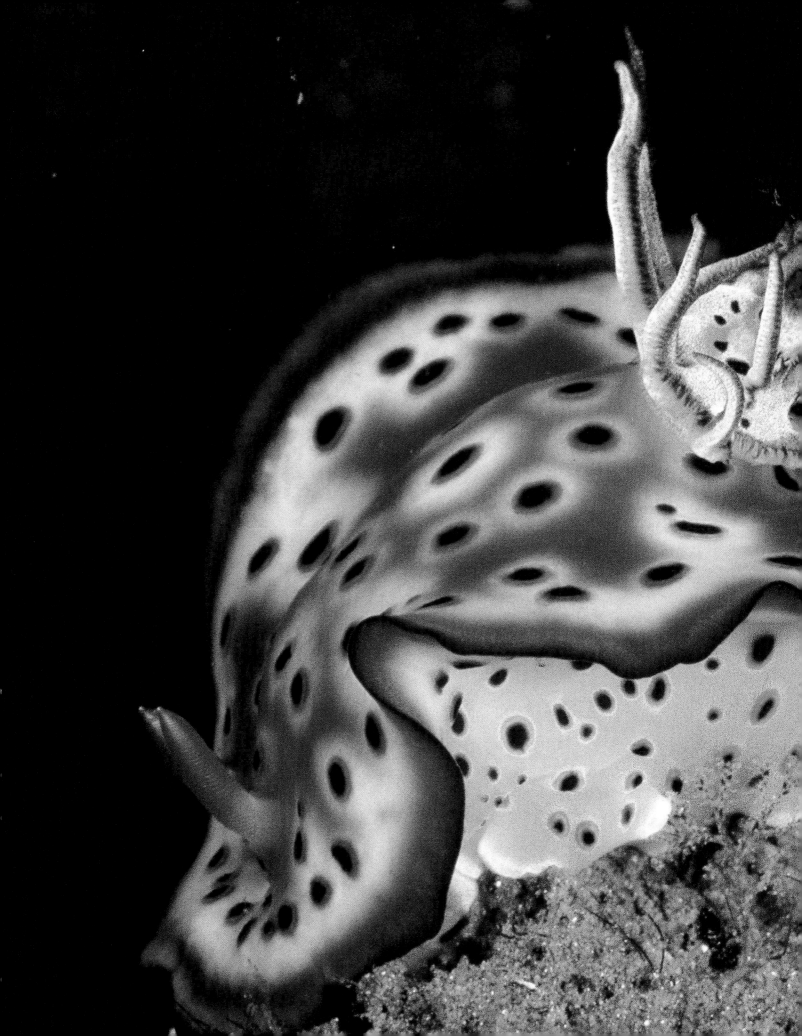

Soft-Bodied Critters

Known mostly for their pretty shells, the soft-bodied critters are called MOLLUSKS. Some—snails and winkles and whelks—have one shell and crawl around on a slick, smooth foot. Others—scallops, oysters, mussels, and clams—have two shells.

MOON SNAIL

The brightly colored sea slug, called a nudibranch, has no shell at all. Gills and eyestalks up, it glides along, belly down, scouting for a meal.

GIANT CLAM

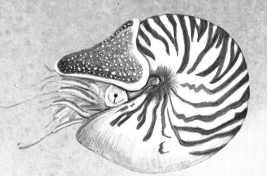

NAUTILUS

Of all the mollusks, none can move as fast as octopus and squid. Most have incredible eyes, big brains, and tentacles with suction cups. Some, such as the young squid relative in the photograph, can signal pals by changing skin color in a flash from pale to dark to speckled or even striped. Imagine being able to change the way you look in an instant. Many of these incredible suckers—octopus and squid—are very small. You could hold a hundred in your arms. But one kind, the giant squid, is longer than a school bus and could hold a hundred of you quite easily.

OCTOPUS

SQUID

Animals with Jointed Legs

Critters with legs and arms and knees are called ARTHROPODS. Some have wings like bugs and flies, most have eyes, and nearly all are small. Their cousins in the sea are also on the small side, which can make them hard to find. But close-up, you'll see that even little shrimp can be quite beautiful. The two tiny shrimp in the photograph can move with style, though mostly they prefer to hide away from hungry fish who might crunch them into lunch.

LOBSTER

AMPHIPOD

CRAB

SHRIMP ▶

How would you like to carry your house on your back? The jointed-legged hermit crab

SEA SPIDER

is doing just that! Thousands of kinds of crabs live in the sea. Some swim in the open ocean with paddle-like legs. Others make their homes in sandy burrows or rocky crevices. Others live in seaweed or ride on the backs of other animals, such as sand dollars and sea cucumbers. Some crabs even live inside oysters and sea urchins! But hermit crabs have found a way to stay at home and move around at the same time. When they are still very small, they crawl into an empty seashell and then walk away with it. Like kids who outgrow their clothes, as one of these critters gets bigger it must change its too-tight shell for a larger one.

HORSESHOE
CRAB

HERMIT CRAB ▶

Spiny-Skinned Critters

Starfish are not fish, but they are shaped like stars, with five arms and beautiful, bumpy skin. The spiny-skinned critters called ECHINODERMS also include sand dollars, urchins, and even lumpy sea cucumbers. Starfish glide along rocks or sand on dozens of tiny, soft, tubular feet that you can see if you turn a starfish upside down.

PURPLE SEA URCHIN

How does it eat? With its mouth, of course! It's right in the center of the star, underneath. Imagine what it must be like to move along the ground, ready to wrap your arms around little clams and other small creatures to gobble them up.

BRITTLE STAR

◄ STARFISH

Like their cousins the starfish and other spiny-skinned critters, the many-armed sea lilies, such as the one in the photograph, are based on the number five. Some have ten arms, others have more, but they join at the center around the mouth in a starlike pattern. Some sea lilies swim; others simply crawl from place to place. They lift their feathery arms to gather very small creatures that flow past in the surrounding sea.

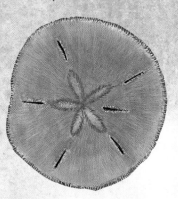

SAND DOLLAR

BASKET STAR

SEA CUCUMBER

SEA LILY ▶

Stiff-Backed Creatures

Fish, turtles, birds, frogs, dogs, whales, and people are cousins of the sea squirts in the photograph. All these critters are called **CHORDATES**. Chordates have a stiff but bendable rod and a hollow nerve cord running down their back. Most have bones, although sea squirts don't. As babies they look a lot like little fish. Sea squirts slurp water in one opening and squirt it out another, meanwhile straining out drifting morsels of food. Some sit in one place most of their lives, but others swim, gilding around alone or with others in long chains. In the deep sea, some flash, sparkle, and glow in the dark with their own built-in lights.

SEA SQUIRT

SALP

AMPHIOXUS

If you come face-to-face with the creatures in the photograph, you may wonder what they are. At the same time, they may be wondering what you are! After all, fish are curious. Like you, they have eyes, a brain, a heart, and very sensitive skin. Everyone knows fish have bones—even eels. Like other fish, eels have gills through which they breathe, and they live in the water all their lives. They have no arms or legs, but when they leave the reef to swim around, they can move fast by using their strong muscles and rippling fins. There are more kinds of fish—about 25,000—than all other kinds of animals with bones combined.

PENGUIN

RAY

MORAY EELS ▶

What's that critter swimming over the coral reef? Not a fish, not a turtle, not a sea squirt. It's a diver, someone like you. Fish and dolphins and whales can't walk around on the land or ride in a car, but people can go into the sea. Like seals and whales, people don't have gills, but by taking a deep breath and holding it, humans can dive. With a special scuba air tank, we can take air underwater with us. Then, for a while, we can explore places and see creatures who are at home there all the time. Perhaps you would like to dive into the sea and meet these critters personally.

DOLPHIN

TURTLE

The Sea Critters' Family Tree

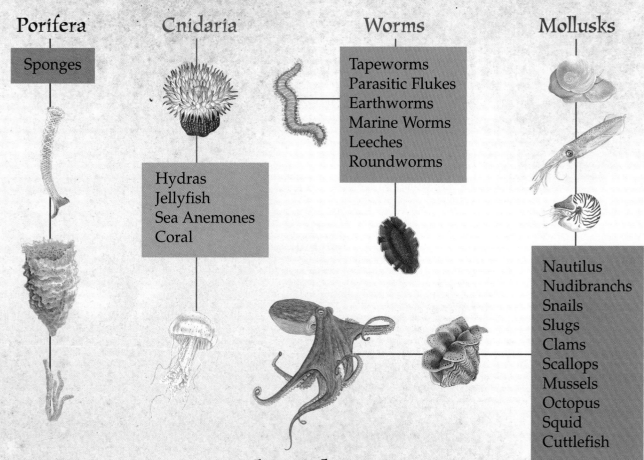

Porifera

Sponges

Cnidaria

Hydras
Jellyfish
Sea Anemones
Coral

Worms

Tapeworms
Parasitic Flukes
Earthworms
Marine Worms
Leeches
Roundworms

Mollusks

Nautilus
Nudibranchs
Snails
Slugs
Clams
Scallops
Mussels
Octopus
Squid
Cuttlefish

Note to Parents and Teachers

Creatures in the sea are wonderfully diverse, much more so than those on land. Only one of 30 or so major divisions of animal life, the chordates, includes animals with backbones. Yet many people, when they think of animals, tend to focus on one branch of the chordates—the vertebrates, which includes humans as well as other mammals, birds, fish, amphibians, and reptiles.

The division that includes insects—the arthropods—has more known species than any other. But less than 5 percent of the ocean has been explored, and some other groups of life, especially several categories lumped together here as worms, remain largely unknown.

Discoveries in recent years include several new phyla of animals and a new kingdom of microbial life, the *Archeae*. As exploration continues, new insights will surely follow concerning the diversity and nature of life on Earth, especially in the sea.

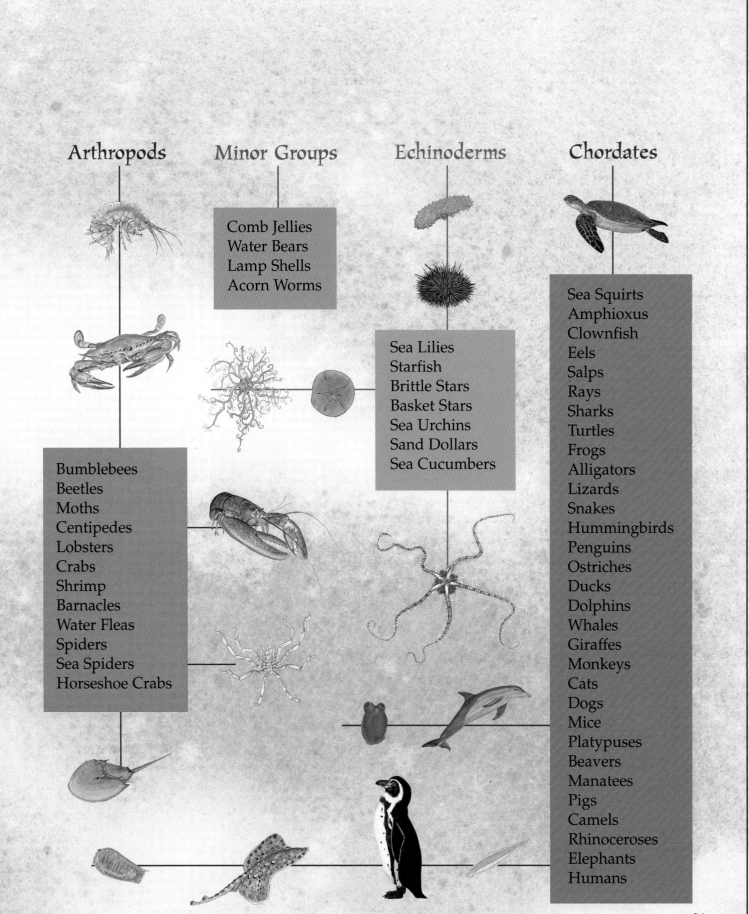

Arthropods

Bumblebees
Beetles
Moths
Centipedes
Lobsters
Crabs
Shrimp
Barnacles
Water Fleas
Spiders
Sea Spiders
Horseshoe Crabs

Minor Groups

Comb Jellies
Water Bears
Lamp Shells
Acorn Worms

Echinoderms

Sea Lilies
Starfish
Brittle Stars
Basket Stars
Sea Urchins
Sand Dollars
Sea Cucumbers

Chordates

Sea Squirts
Amphioxus
Clownfish
Eels
Salps
Rays
Sharks
Turtles
Frogs
Alligators
Lizards
Snakes
Hummingbirds
Penguins
Ostriches
Ducks
Dolphins
Whales
Giraffes
Monkeys
Cats
Dogs
Mice
Platypuses
Beavers
Manatees
Pigs
Camels
Rhinoceroses
Elephants
Humans

NATALIE FOBES

Sylvia A. Earle is a marine

biologist, author, lecturer, and ocean explorer. She has been the National Geographic Society's Explorer-in-Residence since 1998. As part of the Sustainable Seas Expeditions launched in 1998 with Society support, Earle plans to dive in all 12 U.S. marine sanctuaries. Called "Her Deepness" by the *New York Times*, Sylvia Earle has a B.S. from Florida State University and a Ph.D. from Duke University, as well as numerous honorary doctorates. When not underwater, Sylvia Earle lives in Oakland, California.

Wolcott Henry is an

underwater photographer who has explored coral reef areas all over the world, including Indonesia, Papua New Guinea, the Galápagos Islands, Hawaii, and the Florida Keys. He is president of the Curtis and Edith Munson Foundation, an organization that supports marine conservation in North America. Henry's photographs are often used by nonprofit groups to communicate the importance of ocean life. He lives in Washington, D.C.